D0997337

Voices of Africa

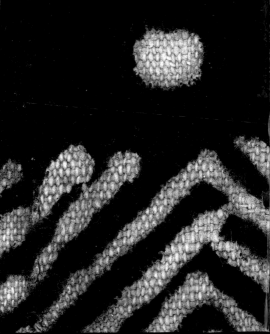

Voices

of

Africa

• • • •

Its Words
and People

Andrews McMeel
Publishing

Kansas City

Voices
of Africa: Its
Words and People
copyright © 1998 by
Armand Eisen. All rights re-
served. Printed in Hong Kong. No
part of this book may be used or repro-
duced in any manner whatsoever without
written permission except in the case of reprints in
the context of reviews. For information write Andrews
McMeel Publishing, an Andrews McMeel Universal company,
4520 Main Street, Kansas City, Missouri 64111.

www.andrewsmcmeel.com

ISBN: 0-8362-6793-1

Library of Congress Catalog Card Number:
98-84251

Biographies based on *Worldwide Interesting
People: 162 History Makers of African
Descent* © 1992 George L. Lee by
permission of McFarland &
Company, Inc., Pub-
lishers, Jefferson,
North Carolina
28640.

Voices

of

Africa

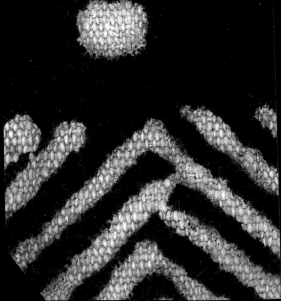

The many words of wisdom emanating from Africa underline a fiercely spiritual pride. The countless examples of courage, intelligence, and trailblazing have helped shape the continent's destiny, which has been at times full of violence and struggle, but always close-knit, community oriented, and colorful. Like the variety of its climate—desert, ocean, mountain, and valley—the African experience has known highs and lows, joys and sorrows, and breathtaking displays of daring and courage in its quest to be free and untamed.

Documented here are the words and deeds of the people who have made up the very fiber of Africa's multifaceted life. Scholars, poets, political leaders, and prisoners—all have had a part in creating Africa's bold tapestry. Their poignant words, proverbs, and concerns for the public good come from every corner of the continent, and speak not only to her own tribes and newly independent nations, but to people struggling for freedom and independence all over the globe.

All of us [black people] are bound to Mother Africa by invisible but tenacious bonds. She has nurtured the deepest things in us blacks. All of us have roots that go deep into the warm soil of Africa, so that no matter how long and traumatic our separation from our ancestral

home has been, there are things
we are often unable to articulate
but which we feel in our very
bones, things which make us dif-
ferent from others who have not
suckled the breasts of our mother,
Africa.

—Desmond Tutu

Words are sweet, but they
never take the place of food.

—Ibo proverb

He who treats you as himself
does you no injustice.

—Lon proverb

Blessed are the common people. God loves them; that is why he made millions of them.

—Nnamdi Azikwe

Master Strategist:
King Piankhi
of Nubia

For many years, Egypt's pharaohs had dominated surrounding nations and forced them to make tribute payments, in money and slaves, to underwrite Egypt's massive construction projects. Proud King Piankhi of Nubia was also forced to submit, but he made wise use of these years. He secretly mustered and trained a huge army and thoroughly studied defenses of Egypt's ports and towns. In 750 B.C., Piankhi marched his troops into Memphis, the capital of Egypt, masqueraded as tribute slaves for the pharaoh. Once there, Egypt fell under the complete mastery and control of "The Black King."

We will water the thorn for
the sake of the rose.

—Kanem proverb

The lack of knowledge is
darker than night.

—African proverb

Despair is the one sin that
cannot be forgiven.

—Ngũgĩ Wa Thiong'o

A powerful friend becomes
a powerful enemy.

—Ethiopian proverb

There are times when even the greatest tactician in diplomatic cunning is outclassed in his own game. It is then that he discovers that all that he thought he had gained is but loss, and that what is left of national honor and dignity is but the shadow of an illustrious past that is gone forever, or of a potentially great future that will never come.

—Obafemi Awolowo

The Master:
Juan Latino

Juan Latino was a black African slave born in Guinea in 1516. He was taken to Spain at age twelve to work in the household of the Duke de Sesa. The duke thought Juan so bright, he sent him to school and to the University of Granada. Juan Latino showed such talent that he became a tutor to noble families. Around age fifty, he returned to the university as a professor of poetry. His most famous poem, "The Austriad," which detailed his friend Don Juan of Austria's exploits against the Turks in the Battle of Lepanto, brought Juan Latino honor and respect. From slave boy to literary hero, Juan Latino died at the ripe age of eighty-three.

Sorrow is like rice in the store; if a basketful is removed every day, it will come to an end at last.

—Somali proverb

Men have no better guidance
than examples and facts
proved by experience.

—Muhammad 'Abduh

When God wills that an event
will occur, He sets the causes
that will lead to it.

—Babikir Badri

24

By the time the fool has
learned the game, the players
have dispersed.

—Ashanti proverb

25

Run, as hard as a wild beast if
you will, but you won't get
any reward greater than that
destined for you.

—Egyptian proverb

God! I am in your hands!
What you say will happen!
Nothing baffles you!

—Ibo prayer

The real malady is fear of life,
not death.

—Naguib Mahfouz

The fool is thirsty in the
midst of water.

—Ethiopian proverb

Joseph Cinque

Joseph Cinque, born in 1811, was at the center of one of the most daring sea epics. In 1839, he was captured in Africa and sold into slavery in Cuba. Aboard the slave ship *Amistad*, bound for the island of Principe, Cinque organized his fellow slaves in a successful revolt against the crew.

Cinque ordered the captain to return him to Africa, but the captain tricked him and headed toward America, where the United States Navy seized the ship. The Spanish insisted the *Amistad* be returned to them, but the American courts refused. Then the American abolitionist movement came to the aid of Cinque and the other slaves in their trial in Connecticut. The *Amistad* case went all the way to the U.S. Supreme Court, and John Quincy Adams himself defended Cinque and his companions. On March 9, 1841, the court granted freedom to Joseph Cinque and his fellow slaves.

Everybody loves a fool, but
nobody wants him for a son.

—Malinke proverb

He who speaks to termite hills
will not get any sense
out of them.

—'Abdiliaahi Muuse

The road to freedom is full of
thorns and fire, yet happy is
he who follows it!

—Aminu Kano

Ingratitude is sooner or later
fatal to its author.

—Twi proverb

I have one abiding religion—
human liberty.

—Wole Soyinka

Father of African Education:
Dr. James E. K. Aggrey

Dr. James Aggrey, the son of a Fanti tribe chief, was born in Gold Coast (now Ghana) in 1872. He was educated at a white mission and was already a teacher by age fifteen. Aggrey, as secretary of the Aborigines Rights Protective Association, forced the defeat of an English bill that proposed to take the land away from Africans. Aggrey then enrolled at Livingstone College in North Carolina, where he later taught, and established the first American Negro credit union. After two decades in America, he returned to Gold Coast to teach Africans the importance of education and national and ethnic pride.

He who is guilty is the one
that has much to say.

—Ashanti proverb

Hate has no medicine.

—Ghanaian proverb

Until the enemy comes to attack me in my camp, and I hear the fusillade and I see them with my eyes, not until then shall I send out my army in order of battle.

—Menelik

Money is sharper than
a sword.

—Ashanti proverb

Idleness leads to relaxation, sooner or later bringing about ideological and material corruption, accompanied by lack of discipline, anarchy, chaos, and defeat.

—Samora Machel

He who hates, hates himself.

—Zulu proverb

Anyone who wants to be a
leader must be the servant,
not the boss, of those he
wants to serve.

—Aminu Kano

One falsehood spoils a
thousand truths.

—Ashanti proverb

When a chap is in love, he will go out in all kinds of weather to keep an appointment with his beloved. Love can be demanding, in fact more demanding than law. It has its own imperatives—think of a mother sitting by the bedside of a sick child through the night, impelled only by love. Nothing is too much trouble for love.

—Desmond Tutu

Pride only goes
the length one can spit.

—Congo proverb

As long as one people sit on another and are deaf to their cry, so long will understanding and peace elude all of us.

—Chinua Achebe

The Lion of Swaziland:
King Sobhuza II

A popular king and diplomat, Sobhuza II was crowned King of Swaziland in 1921 at age twenty-two and ruled the tiny British protectorate for sixty years. He is said to have had one hundred wives and more than five hundred children! When Swaziland won independence from Great Britain in 1968, Sobhuza vowed to return lands seized by white settlers to their rightful Swazi owners. At his coronation, only 37 percent of the land belonged to Swazis; by the time of his death in 1982, 73 percent had been restored.

King Sobhuza, dearly loved by his people, was listed in the Swaziland phone directory simply as "His Majesty."

The rain does not recognize
anyone as a friend; it
drenches all equally.

—Ibo proverb

The most potent weapon in
the hands of the oppressor is
the mind of the oppressed.

—Steve Biko

We shall be free only together, black and white. We shall survive only together, black and white. We can be human only together, black and white.

—Desmond Tutu

You are beautiful; but learn
to work, for you cannot eat
your beauty.

—Congo proverb

Humiliation, slavery, fear
have perverted us to the
bone; we no longer look like
men. . . . Men must be granted
the respect due to them.

—Mohammed Dib

Work is the medicine
for poverty.

—Yoruba proverb

A federal system of government is always full of problems and difficulties, but so is democracy, because the art of persuasion is much more difficult than a dictatorship, though in the long run more rewarding and satisfying.

—Abu Bakar Tafawa Balewa

Sticks in a bundle are
unbreakable.

—Bondei proverb

59

A chattering bird builds
no nest.

—Cameroon proverb

An African writer who really wants to interpret the African scene has to write in three dimensions at once. There is the private life, the social life, and what you may call the supernatural.

—Elechi Amadi

The greatest obstacle to love is fear. It has been the source of all defects in human behavior throughout the ages.

—Mahmoud Mohammed Taha

When the mouse laughs at the cat, there is a hole nearby.

—Benin proverb

You are either alive and
proud, or you are dead,
and when you are dead, you
can't care anyway.

—Steve Biko

When the brothers fight to death, a stranger inherits their father's estate.

—Ibo proverb

Saint of the Ages:
Blessed Martin de Porres

Blessed Martin, the illegitimate child of a Spanish nobleman and an ex-slave, was born in Peru in 1579. The boy, abandoned by his father, ended up as a servant in a convent, where he performed menial labor, begged, and tended to the sick and poor. He became a monk at age twenty-four, and earned a loyal following because of his charity and healing touch. Three hundred and twenty-three years later, in 1962, Pope John XXIII canonized Blessed Martin, the fifth black saint, whose devotion to the menial earned him the protectorate of the "Saint of the Broom."

It is in seeing the actions of vicious and wicked people and comparing them with what my conscience tells me regarding such actions that I have learned what I ought to avoid and what I ought to do. The wise and prudent man will draw a useful lesson even from poison itself.

—Lokman

If you understand the begin-
ning well, the end will not
trouble you.

—Ashanti proverb

Always being in a hurry does not prevent death, neither does going slowly prevent living.

—Ibo proverb

The real tragedy is that we're all human beings, and human beings have a sense of dignity. Any domination by one human over another leads to a loss of some part of his dignity. Is one's dignity that big it can be crumbled away like that?

—Yusuf Idris

Hope is the pillar of
the world.

—Proverb

Happiness can grow from
only a little contentment.

—Pygmy proverb

Our children may learn about heroes of the past. Our task is to make ourselves architects of the future.

—Jomo Kenyatta

Where there is no shame,
there is no honor.

—Congo proverb

Prize-Winning Trailblazer:
Albert Luthuli

Born in Rhodesia in 1900, Luthuli began his career as a humble teacher. But at age thirty-five, he started on his rise to prominence when he became chief of his Zulu tribe. In 1945, Luthuli joined the African National Congress and was later elected to lead it. In this capacity, he served as the voice for South Africa's majority black population trying to break free from the yoke of apartheid. The white South African government even charged him with treason in 1956, but he was acquitted. For his efforts to rid South Africa of apartheid's oppression, Luthuli was awarded the 1960 Nobel Peace Prize. He died seven years later.

Copying everyone else
all the time, the monkey
one day cut his throat.

—Zulu proverb

My humanity is bound up in yours, for we can only be human together.

—Desmond Tutu

This book
was designed by
BTD/Sabrina Bowers
and typeset in
Lunatix Bold.